The Bereavement Code

How To Survive Grief and Move Beyond the Loss of a Loved One

Jack Wilson

CONTENTS

JACK WILSON

THE VACANT ROOM

I saw death stalking the valley every now and then. There were no houses, churches or schools that it hadn't visited. Each passing day, I sensed it mocking me from the outside, just waiting for the right time. And that time came in the most unexpected of hours!

Death wasn't kind. In the deep slumbers of the night, it sneaked up on her and snatched the most precious things while I lay beside. It didn't make a sound or cause a scene, it just did what it came to do, without any emotion, in a raw manner. I like to think it didn't even pretend to care.

I remember waking up to her lifeless self. Lying motionless with a half-smile on her face like most of the other days. But I instantly knew something was off. Something felt uneasy, like the brewing of a storm or a tsunami underwater. The hooded vale of death had done its job once again.

The strangest thing is that most of us have witnessed the death of a close one. A relative, a baby in the womb or a kid taken too young. But until it happens to you, you never really know the extent of the damage the remnant left by the deceased causes. The remains of countless memories, the laughter, the smiles, hugs and kisses—unless it happens to you! The death of my wife felt like someone ripped my heart from my chest while I was alive. The pain was too unbearable to feel, let alone write about. I don't recall the first few minutes of it. It all seems like kind of a haze today. But I do remember shaking her body vigorously for signs of life, perhaps just one breath. I remember rushing her to the ER. I remember waiting for the doctors to come out of the emergency room and tell me that it was too late and my worst fear had already happened.

You see, sometimes, we receive signs that predict the future. You take note of them and then plan out things accordingly. With my beloved wife, it was never like this. Death stole up to her unannounced and too early. One day, she was playing with our boys in the backyard, teaching the youngest one the 101s to gardening, and the next moment they were the ones lowering her lifeless soul into the ground. She didn't even get to see the light of that day.

When the reports came back, we were notified that her heart stopped beating around 2 in the morning. I remember waking up from a sound… more like a whisper. I can't exactly say whether it was my wife's voice bidding me goodbye or the mocking of the Grim Reaper, as he used his scythe to cleave my wife's soul from her flesh.

I don't know where it took her, whether she was directed to enter the pearly white gates of heaven or told to climb down the stairs to hell. What I do know is that she was a kind, beautiful, caring and loving partner and wife.

What I also know is that I am left in this vacant room all by myself to cry to sleep every night. I have overcome my grief, for the most part, but some days, it gets really hard not to think about the empty space on the bed or wake up hoping to find her by the bed.

It took me long enough to get a hold of my emotions. I never knew you could cry this much all at once. It was harsh, unannounced and uncalled for. But I accepted it. It took some counseling, emotional support and diversions, but I finally got through it. I succumbed to my new reality, although I never thought I would. I admitted that when the time comes, you have to pack your bags and get going.

There were days when I would fear stepping into the room alone. I just felt her presence and it bothered me. There was this persistent coldness and smell in the room, something no one agreed to, but I knew. I didn't want to get out of bed or leave the house. The bills kept piling up, the boys kept looking to me for support, but I was in a completely different state of mind.

The purpose of this book is to help someone like myself. Someone who thought that the pain was too much to bear. Someone who stopped thinking rationally about anything and everything because nothing seemed to make sense. Someone who kept replaying things a thousand times in his mind, figuring out if there was something he could have done differently to prevent the current state. For days before it was revealed that my wife passed away due to sleep apnea, I kept going over every tiny detail of that day. I thought about the things she ate, her mood and if she had called for me while I slept. I made up scenarios in my head where I changed the outcome of the situation. I blamed myself for several days thinking I could have saved her if I had just rushed her to the hospital earlier and whatnot.

So if you are anything like me and struggling to get by each day, then I hope my journey to a more grateful and happier me inspires you and leads you in the right direction. I hope you can relate to the struggles I went through and see through those tough days and dark and lonely nights. I hope that you find the strength within you to move on and move forward.

1 THE ACT OF GRIEVING

Since this book is going to be about grief, bereavement and how to overcome the emotional turmoil that most of us are left in, it only makes sense if we start right from the basics. You will be astonished to know the literal meaning of the word grief and where it originates from. Let's take a look!

It was some 800 years ago when the word grief was first used in the English language to denote hardship, pain or suffering. Don't we feel excruciating pain when a beloved dies?

It was derived from the Old French word of the same spelling denoting some misfortune or injustice. Doesn't it feel unjust when someone we love passes away?

Another word in Old French has the same origin—grever, which means to afflict, burden or oppress. Again, right on point: All of a sudden your life starts to feel like a burden so hard to bear.

The French language took these words from the Latin word gravare, which means to make heavy or weighty. It usually is used when describing the heaviness of one's heart and I couldn't agree more. Grief does feel like a burden our hearts carry until we learn how to relieve ourselves from it.

Understanding Bereavement

That is grief. It can be expressed over things other than death, such as retiring from work, moving away from family, parting of lovers, etc. So the right term for the kind of loss and grief you are going through is bereavement.

What does bereavement mean?

There have been multiple attempts to explain it but everyone seems to be confused. Losing someone close to our hearts is like an amputation. The pain just never leaves and the constant reminder of that face, a space in the house, a wardrobe and accessories never leave the mind. The term bereavement comes from the word reave which means to take away by violence or carry off. It feels like a non-surgical ripping of the heart in an unsanitary manner without anesthesia. Too clinical, right? Well, that is how it felt to me, and anyone who has been through such a loss would probably agree, at least in some fashion.

The most apt definition of the term bereavement comes from Dr. Elisabeth Kübler-Ross's book (Kübler-Ross, On Death and Dying, 1969). She suggests that it is the time of mourning after the death of a loved one. She talks about bereavement through the 5 stages of grief, starting with denial and ending with acceptance. Her theory is still considered one of the most original takes on the term bereavement and offers us a template for grieving.

But as time has passed and more psychologists began to research further into people's experiences of grief, they came to the realization that the stages of grief were nothing but a controlling way of teaching us how to grieve, when in reality, everyone had their own methods of grieving and moving on. Although Kübler-Ross succeeded in capturing the essence of the emotions and turmoil a mourner goes through, she still failed to be practical. Many argued that grief doesn't follow a checklist and not everyone experiences all the stages of grief. There was also a clash of opinions on how long each stage lasts, as there isn't a one-size-fits-all solution to the problem.

Later, on her deathbed, Dr. Kübler-Ross partnered with David Kessler and wrote another book (Kübler-Ross & Kessler, On Grief and Grieving, 2005). They explained that she never intended to force the five stages in a systematic order. She agreed that grief was never meant to be neat, predictable or stagnant. Instead, it is supposed to be complex, hurtful and a process that some never fully recover from. In her own words, the five stages were "never meant to help tuck messy emotions into neat packages."

A Revised Take on the Stages of Grief

A revised take on the existing theory was put forward by George A. Bonanno, professor of clinical psychology at the Teachers College at Columbia University. He presented his contradictory views about the stages of grief in his book, The Other Side of Sadness: What the New Science of Bereavement Tells Us About Life After Loss. Dr. Bonanno's experimental research proposed, first, that there is no scientific evidence to prove that the process of grieving is similar for everyone and, second, that not everyone goes through the five stages of grief (Bonanno, 2009).

According to Bonanno, mourners represent unique patterns of grief throughout time. The emotions can range from overwhelming feelings to no feelings at all and can also happen simultaneously. One minute you feel fine and the next minute you don't. He also believes that the first two years after the death of a loved one are the most crucial to get through, and then the feelings of grief begin to subdue as time goes by. The feelings of intense pain eventually weaken with time, especially after the first few weeks of death. He also suggested that humans are born with the capacity to get over anything with time and routine activities. Our bodies are designed to combat trauma and regain equilibrium. Basically, our bodies, like us, keep growing. The brain keeps making new memories that leave little space for the existing information and thus the uncontrollability of the situation comes under control as we return to mundane activities.

I personally agree with the necessity to modify the definition tied with the five stages. A lot of times, others expect the mourner to just wait for it or move past the loss. People come to us to tell us that time heals all and everything will be fine eventually, we just need to stay strong. This assumption, although right, is hard to process and apply in real life. Such implications suggest that a mourner is nothing but a passive human being, waiting for the course of emotions to die down and submit to a fractured system of grief for a set period of time without having any control over how they feel. Now that you come to think of it in this way, it seems kind of stupid, doesn't it? Impractical, to be more precise, as we all express grief differently.

The 5 Stages of Grief

Having talked about it several times in the section above, you might be wondering what the five stages are. Many of us are familiar with these but don't actually understand the significance each stage holds and why we need to pass through them (or maybe not all). Undoubtedly, some of them help us move forward with life, enabling us to accept and control the situation we are in. Clearly, you can't stay in bed your whole life or cry about your loss with every other person you meet. One day, you will have to get out and face the world as an independent individual who has been through some tough times but has learned to progress towards a less painful tomorrow.

One key thing to note is that throughout the time of grief, there is a possibility that one might regress to a previous stage of loss. For instance, you may think that you have gotten over your anger and moved passed that stage, but something or someone might remind you of a trigger that takes you back to being angry or makes you feel guilty for not doing enough. Listen to me: it is okay if that happens. No one is going to judge you over how you choose to mend yourself back together. No one is going to question how long you will take to get back to normal. So don't try to rush through the grieving process, thinking the sooner you pass it, the easier it will get to control your life.

Before I begin, remember that every individual experiences and expresses grief differently. Some wear it proudly on their sleeves and aren't emotional when talking about it while others just keep it all bottled up and rarely cry or talk about it. During each stage, you will notice a thread of clinging hope that keeps on emerging. Your goal is to tug on it as hard as you can because that is the one thing that is going to get you through.

Stage 1: Denial

When I lost my wife, from the moment I found her lifeless on the bed to the minute the doctors came out of the ER to tell us that she was no more, I was in complete shock and disbelief. There was no way it was happening to me. I was sure that the doctors had made some mistakes or that I was dreaming a terrible dream.

Sometimes, when a death occurs out of the blue, it can take us by surprise. It can take us some time to register our new reality because we don't want to accept it. This first stage is called denial. You deny that the person you just talked to over the phone an hour ago is no longer. You deny that something so heinous and nerve-shattering can happen to you.

You must understand that denial is acceptable and is just an attempt by our brain to process the loss and trauma. It is fine if it takes you hours to a day to absorb and understand it. During this stage, we reflect on the experiences and cherished moments we spent together and because of that, it feels impossible to move forward. The memories are raw and hurtful and that is what makes it harder for our brain to register them completely. Since the one who departed was someone close, there can be a lot of information to process through, which is why we are our most vulnerable during this stage.

Stage 2: Anger

Although a negative emotion, anger is one of the most crucial phases of any grieving process. The more anger you feel or experience, the sooner it will begin to dissipate. Think of it as cleansing yourself of all the bad emotions, guilt, and negativity from your system. The sooner it is out, the sooner you will find peace. Anger is also important when it comes to helping you heal. Anger can have no limits. Some days you might feel like burning the whole house down and some days it may seem manageable. You might feel angry for a number of reasons. You might feel anger because the deceased never gave you a chance to say goodbye. You might be angry at yourself for not being there for them or you might feel angry over others and how fast they have come to terms with the death and moved on.

When I was in mourning and started going back to work, I detested the way my colleagues would just spend all day laughing, chit-chatting or gossiping while I felt so lost and incomplete. I felt angry over the way they treated me. I wanted them to feel some empathy towards me. But I was wrong. They had every reason to be who they were because they weren't grieving. They hadn't lost someone as I did. So expecting them to shower me with favors, sympathy, and support was just out of the question. When I saw it from this perspective, I began to better channel and control my anger.

Keep in mind that the reason you are angry with yourself or others is that deep down you are hurting. You are in pain and that is okay. You feel abandoned, deserted and heartbroken. But that doesn't mean that you go around expecting favors or hoping that everyone should be on the same page as you.

Stage 3: Bargaining

People who have seen someone close to them suffer through an illness bargain with God all the time to spare them from it. And even after it happens, the bargaining doesn't stop. There were days when I would have conversations with myself and God that I would dedicate my whole life to volunteering for kids or senior citizens or that I would change my habits, be a better human being, a better citizen, kinder, more caring, more devoted and whatnot if only he would return my wife back. I prayed to God to take it all away and wake me up from this horrendous nightmare. But nothing of that sort happened.

After we lose someone, bargaining seems like a form of truce we are willing to make with the higher power. We keep walking through mazes of what-ifs, and "if only" statements, hoping that our lives will return to how they were. We keep thinking if only we had found the disease earlier, recognized the symptoms, talked with someone sooner before their life ended… If only this, if only that. We even bargain with the amount of pain we experience. After all, wouldn't you give anything to not feel like this? If there was some way to walk out of this pain and anguish, wouldn't you be the first one to buy tickets to it too?

The stage of bargaining allows us to come to terms with our situation. We begin to move forward from the denial stage and begin to accept what has happened. Therefore, even when we are bargaining for our lives back, we are also accepting that something traumatic has occurred. This realization alone is a step forward, as now we can move onto finding the much-needed motivation to see through.

Stage 4: Depression

This stage can happen at different intervals for different people. For me, it happened right after denial. There were constant sadness and stress. Since most of the household tasks were my wife's, attempting to do them was in itself stressful. I wouldn't want to get out of bed and feel like a complete failure. I would rather cry about these responsibilities or delay them until the very last minute. I avoided going out or meeting friends and family over the holidays because I felt that no one understood my grief. The happier everyone around me seemed, the more depressed I became. Thoughts about self-harm and suicide started to cross my mind every now and then. I just hated the state I was in, and at that time it seemed that there was no way I was going to get out of it. But it was all a phase. The pain subdued, the feelings disappeared. I began to do things just like my wife used to do them. I was no longer mentally incapacitated. With time, countless mistakes and pushes from my family and friends, I came out stronger than ever. I felt more empowered, more in control of my decisions, less anxious about trying new things—ultimately overcoming depression and coming back to life.

This stage is an important stage because it takes us into the deepest pits of darkness and loneliness so that we can come out stronger. You must have heard the saying that only when we are at our lowest are we able to rise back up. It holds true in my case. Had I not hit rock bottom, I would have never gathered the strength to get back up. For me, it happened in just one instant. I remember that I hadn't bathed in three days, spent most of the time in bed drinking and neglected all the household chores because I was ready to give up. There seemed no point in trying; nothing was ever going to get better. But the fourth day, I just told myself I had to get out of bed, for my own health and for the sake of my kids. After all, they too had lost someone close to them. Being kids, they looked up to me and expected me to comfort them and not the other way around.

So I decided I wouldn't cry anymore. I would seek therapy if needed and live for them. That day for me marks a milestone that I completed. A milestone where I decided I was going to be a better dad, a better human being, a better friend and a better supporter. The point is that you shouldn't try to escape this stage as it is indeed needed. If you are anywhere near this stage or already sunken into it, see it as a positive thing. Things are only going to get better from this point onwards.

Stage 5: Acceptance

Before I even delve into this, let's get one thing very clear: Acceptance doesn't mean that everything is ok. You may get over the sadness but never be fully out of it. You may never feel like before but still go on with your life. The idea behind this stage is coming to terms with the death sanely. This phase is about acknowledging the death and that it has happened. There is no way life can be like before. It is accepting that your soul mate or loved one has departed this earth physically and nothing you do or don't do will affect them anymore. It is about adjusting to your new normal and living in that reality. It is about allowing yourself to move forward without any guilt, anger, or regrets. It is about freeing yourself from all the doubts you have about yourself. It is about trying new things—things you never thought you would do—and excelling in them. It is about remembering your loved one and not breaking down. It is about helping others seek comfort and closure the same way you did. It is about getting up every day with new hope and inspiration to live. It is all those things and much more than just blatantly accepting that someone important from your life has left for the next world.

2 HOW GRIEF AFFECTS YOU

The experience of grief causes us to question our sanity. Sometimes we see our lost loved ones in a crowded space and other times in our dreams. Some mourners suffering from chronic symptoms of grief may even begin to abstractly question their reason for being alive. The symptoms of grief, whether physical, emotional or mental must never be avoided or looked down upon, as they can have a significant impact on the bereaved. Loss of weight, disrupted sleep patterns, poor eating habits, fogginess or forgetfulness are all signs that suggest a deeper issue that must be handled with love and care.

Therefore, we shall look at some of the most commonly associated symptoms of grief and bereavement. Whether you notice these in yourself or someone you deeply care about, don't leave these unattended or think that they will go away on their own. Technically they should and mostly they do, but it isn't the case for everyone. Thus, it is always advisable to address them, acknowledge them and motivate yourself to move past them.

Emotionally

Emotional stress is perceived by the body as a physical threat. The body goes into turbocharging and releases the stress hormone cortisol, which can increase blood pressure and cause other medical conditions like headaches, pain or lowered immune resistance.

Depression and Emptiness

Depression or the feelings of emptiness strike when we come to terms with the death of a loved one. We feel empty inside, sad or constantly depressed with a bad mood, especially during the first few weeks after the death. However, we must understand that depression is also the stage after which the true healing begins. Just keep it in mind that you will probably feel a decline in the feelings of loneliness and sadness as time passes. If not, then you must consult someone about it and see if you need some counseling or therapy.

Anger

Feeling angry over your loss or the injustice done to you is a very natural reaction. You might begin to feel jealous of others who are going on about their lives or at the lack of understanding from everyone around you. No matter how it feels, anger must always be expressed. Internalizing your anger can lead to bigger problems for you, so don't try to bottle it up! Just be sure to do it in a way that doesn't harm yourself or others.

Fear

People who relied on the deceased for everything big and small will have trouble moving on. They often live in constant fear of attempting new things because they now have to take control of their lives. Just know that the first few steps will be the hardest to take. With time, you will find your balance and learn to handle things your way. I know, I did.

Physically

Physical changes and effects are the easiest to spot. It is surprising how grief affects our bodies and physicality (Romm, Understanding How Grief Weakens the Body, 2014). Some of the most noticeable changes include:

Fatigue

Exhaustion is a common complaint of the mourner. Sometimes it is just the unwillingness to get out of bed and other times the saturation of the brain that makes us think that we are exhausted. It is acceptable to feel that way since the constant array of memories that play like a film in your mind can cause fatigue. You may also feel like you are always short of a nap or feel run down. And when you do put your head down for sleep, it doesn't really come that easily, only adding to the level of fatigue. Even if you are getting sound sleep and still feel exhausted, it can be the emotional strain you are going through that's causing your brain to feel numb or tired.

Sleep Problems

Sleep is essential to help the brain and body take a timeout. But you won't be getting much during the first few days after the death. There will always be guests coming over for condolences, the preparation for the funeral, etc. They will keep you on your toes all day long. Isn't it ironic that the one person whom everyone should be offering comfort is usually the one running around the house and taking care of all the arrangements? If it isn't directly bereaved, it usually is the immediate family, who are also grieving but rarely have any time to mourn the loss fully.

Disruption in sleep is a possible outcome and can be frustrating for some. When I was in mourning, sleep felt like a relaxing time to forget about my loss, even if only for a few hours. But whenever I tried to go to sleep, the good and bad memories would hit me like a wave, keeping me up all night reminiscing over the good ones and crying about the bad. Research suggests that insomnia and problems with sleep are a common occurrence during the period of grief (Insomnia, 2017).

Weight Loss

Many bereaved undereat during the first days of mourning. It just feels unfair for some reason. I too had a difficult time with food. I wouldn't want it near me, as that felt like a normal thing and nothing in my life was ever going to be normal again. At least that was what I thought. Surprisingly, my taste buds took a toll too. I couldn't stomach any of the stuff brought to me by family and friends, let alone enjoy it. Since my wife used to do most of the cooking in the house, not having her around, doing the same just felt odd. Besides, there was so much to plan for the funeral, so many preparations to do—move furniture, clean the house, change bedsheets and whatnot that eating was usually the last thing on my mind.

Body Aches and Pains

Pain is a common physical symptom of grief. Many experience pain in the knees, back, joints and even stiffness in the muscles (Chronic Pain, 2018). This is the result of the overwhelming stress our bodies deal with. There is a significant release of stress hormones during the grieving stages. The influx of these hormones stuns the muscles and nerves, making us feel weak and in pain. However, this should only be a temporary state that improves with time. If it doesn't, you might need to take some over-the-counter medications or get it checked by a physician.

Heart Problems

Cardiovascular conditions can be brought on with an excess release of the stress hormones. If someone is already a heart patient, their chances of a stroke or heart attack increase during bereavement, which is why caution must be taken at all times.

There is also a popular phenomenon called the broken heart syndrome that mourners often experience. Despite its name, it is a medical condition in which there is a disruption in the way the heart pumps blood to the other organs. The effects and symptoms are usually similar to that of a heart attack. You may experience shortness of breath, chest and shoulder pain, etc. But there is no need for panic as it usually lasts for a minute or so and is a temporary condition.

Lowered Immunity

Have you ever noticed how you become more susceptible to colds, flu, and fever during the process of grief? It is because your immune system takes a hit during grief. The body experiences a reduction in neutrophil function, which refers to the production of white blood cells by your body. A reduced count of white blood cells in the system makes us prone to diseases as the immune system weakens.

Mentally

Your mental functioning also takes a hit when someone close to you leaves without you on another journey. When we are mourning the loss of someone, we experience flooding of hormones and neurochemicals in our heads. These are the same hormones and neurochemicals that play a crucial role in emotions and affect our prefrontal cortex and limbic system. As a result, the mourner often experiences lapses in memory, headaches, poor clarity and difficulty in multi-tasking, learning, organization and emotional regulation. Other linked physical symptoms can include poor sleep, fatigue, loss of appetite and increased anxiety.

To put it simply, our brain experiences fog when we are overwhelmed with grief. Absorbing everything that is going on around you becomes tougher due to all the hormonal and behavioral changes happening inside the body.

Poor Clarity of Things

Cognitive effects during grief impact our ability to think clearly, pass rational judgments and make wise decisions. We also experience a decline in our problem-solving skills and find ourselves giving up on things rather than trying harder. Bereavement has also been associated with a decline in our memory performance because we have trouble focusing and concentrating (Rosnick, Small, & Burton, 2009).

Forgetfulness

Have you been losing your keys more often? Do you keep forgetting routine chores like taking out the trash, doing the dishes or turning off the shower? Do you forget important dates, events or appointments lately? If so, then you really need to allow yourself some time to fully grieve, as there is no point in functioning like this. You might say that you are at least trying, but you are just torturing yourself with more guilt, regret, and anger. Take a break from work if you don't feel fit mentally. Go someplace for a change in your environment and to think clearly.

Nervousness

Nervousness or anxiety is an aftereffect that some people never get over. When dealing with the task of reassigning chores or taking over someone's place, you are bound to feel nervous. This is usually manifested in ways such as fidgeting, tapping your fingers, feeling sweaty, having numbness or tingling sensations in your hands, etc. You may also find it harder to sit down and think clearly or you may pace back and forth, worried about failing.

Loneliness

This isn't hard to believe, for those of us who have been there. The feelings of loneliness never leave your side and no matter how many people are gathered around you comforting and supporting you, you never get out of that state. At least, not for some time. Again, this is a very natural state to be in. You become distant, seek isolation and feel that there is no one who can connect with you on a similar basis.

Factors Influencing the Grief Process

There are several factors that influence grief. Although we all experience it differently, the nature of it can be relatable. For instance, how close was the deceased to you or how sudden or prolonged was the death? Understanding these factors allows us to understand and cope with our loss in a sane manner. Since there are different factors and many that form connections together, it is no wonder that grief can be so complex and complicated. I will group these factors here into five different groups, based on their nature. What I want you to do is take a pen and paper and circle at least one factor from each group so that by the end of it, you know exactly how your grief looks. Knowing it, owning it and comprehending it is a step forward to dealing with it. The sooner you find your pattern, the easier it will become to manage it.

The Nature of the Loss

- Who was the deceased to you? (A partner, sibling, parent, friend, colleague, etc.)
- What kind of relationship you two had amongst you? (Close, very close, ambivalent, abusive, indifferent)
- Did you suffer through some form of secondary loss after their death? (Social, financial or personal)

The Features of the Mourner

- How good or bad are you at coping with loss and unpredictable situations?
- Do you face them head on or do you run the other way?
- Do you become aggressive?
- Do you indulge in substance abuse like drugs or alcohol?
- Have you been through grief before?
- Are there any specific rituals in your family regarding death?
- Are you emotionally stable and healthy?
- How old are you and how would you define your level of maturity?

Social factors

- What is your economic and occupational status?
- Are you suffering from any work/finances/family-related stress other than death?
- Do you have a support system to help you cope with your loss?
- Are you seeing a therapist, counselor or a support group for your loss?
- Does your culture celebrate the death, remember it with a memorial service or have a funeral?

The Characteristics of the Death

- Was it sudden or accompanied by a prolonged illness?
- Was it violent or quiet and calm?
- Was it expected or unexpected?
- Was it just one person or did more than one person die at the same time?

Once you have a mental picture of your loss, you will be in a much better state to deal with it.

3 ADDRESSING YOUR ANGER, GUILT AND JEALOUSY

In part 3, we shall explore the most common emotions that the bereaved go through but have a difficult time coping with. Emotions like anger, regret, guilt, and jealousy of seeing others having it all and living their blissful lives while you cry to sleep every night are reactions that need to be channeled accordingly. Starting with the most obvious and common emotion, anger, we move onto dealing with the guilt that we sometimes feel and lastly, tackle the most shocking one of all, jealousy. Think of it as setting the base for the following chapter so that you are fully aware of how to manage your emotions in the best manner and come out of the miserable state you are in right now. Again, keep in mind that it is not a race and you have every right to take baby steps to heal yourself out of it.

Dealing With Anger—Why Did This Happen to Me?

Anger, as discussed in part one, is a very normal reaction to a death. We feel it because death happens and we fail to control it. Whether it happened slowly or in an instant, anger is often hard to deal with or manage. The reason we feel so aggravated at times is that, as humans, we are wired to follow a routine. We eat at a set time, sleep at a set time, work 9 to 5, etc. Our brains are designed to follow a set pattern and when something unexpected happens, it just messes up everything in it. Death is something out of our control even though we know no one can escape it. Yet, when it happens, it is no less a shock. Sometimes the anger we feel in response is expressed and other times it isn't.

Expressing anger can result in quarrels and social isolation from friends and family. When this happens, the people trying to help us usually try to back up a little, which can only lead to further misunderstandings and fights. You might interpret it as a lack of support from them and thus further isolate yourself.

The Direction of Your Anger

This is one of the most important questions you need to ask yourself before you start dealing with it: Whom are you so angry at?

Are you angry at the medical professional who wasn't able to save your beloved? Maybe, if he/she had tried harder or been better at what he/she does, your loved one could still be with you. I remember as we were rushing to the ER, the first nurse that checked for my wife's pulse declared her dead right away. I remember being angry and cursing at her in my heart. She should have at least held on to her opinions until a senior doctor attended to her. But I guess she was just doing her job. It is very easy for us to put the blame on someone because it helps our brains make sense of the situation. But I was wrong to think that doctors had the chance to save someone who was already long gone. Nonetheless, if the death did occur due to negligence on the hospital's part, such as mistaking a heart attack for acid reflux or muscle pull and writing out a prescription for it without any tests, that is a completely different matter. Either way, the anger is going to harm you more than help if you continue to harbor it.

Are you angry with yourself? Do you blame yourself for not doing enough? If you think that you might have changed the course of things, then you are partially wrong. For instance, in my case, there was hardly anything I could have done to save my wife. She died in her sleep. He just stopped breathing all of a sudden. But I do remember blaming myself for not noticing the signs and symptoms. Maybe, if I hadn't been such a sound sleeper, I would have noticed the uneven breathing and sought medical help.

If you are a believer in God, then you might direct your anger towards him for taking away your loved one so soon. We often believe that only the old die. We think we and our loved ones still have a long way to go before dying and when it happens out of the blue, we just lose all faith in him. We think he doesn't love us enough which is why he has given us this insufferable pain to deal with.

You may be angry with the disease itself or with the person who caused you the pain. For instance, if your loved one died during an accident, mugging or shooting, then you may be angry with the driver in the other car or the shooter.

If the death resulted from suicide, then you may very well be angry with your loved one for taking his life. You might be angry at him for not coming to you to discuss his state of mind or not telling you about his problems and depression. You might also feel angry for not being there for him or for not being able to support him and deal with his emotions and state of mind in a better way.

Coping With Anger

Now that you are aware of who the target of your anger is, it is time you learn how to manage it. Firstly, know that you don't have to feel the way you feel because it will only add to your suffering. With the implementation of different strategies, there is hope that you will come out of the misery sooner than you think.

Be Expressive About Your Anger

Sometimes it feels like the right thing to do to suppress your emotions. You think that no one around you is going to understand your journey. Therefore, there is no point in telling the whole world about how you feel. You try to put on a happy face and pretend to be strong, especially when you have a family that relies on you to hold it all together. However, there's a drawback to it. The more you suppress your feelings, the more they build up inside. This can lead to blaming others, jealousy, and constant irritation. The worst part: you might resort to counterproductive or unhealthy ways to cope with it. The more you bottle up your feelings, the more frustrated you will get, making it harder for you to come out of this phase of grief.

My take? Accept this anger and let it fuel you toward making things better for yourself and other mourners in the family. Understand where it is coming from and deal with it using healthy ways. For example, I hated the fact that I never suspected sleep apnea in my wife. So instead of being angry with myself, I talked about the disease openly with anyone and everyone that I found. I briefed my friends about it, shared the symptoms of it with fellow colleagues and stressed to my family and relatives to be cautious about their sleeping patterns and observe each other's breathing during sleep. It felt like the right thing to do. Why did I do it? I knew that the disease had won against me once. I wasn't going to let it do it twice. So basically, everyone I cared about the most knew of the disease, its signs and how to cope with it.

The point is, expressing your anger doesn't have to be all about shouting or harming yourself. You can channel it in a positive light and allow it to change its course to sympathy. The way I expressed it felt both comforting and pleasurable. The more I talked about it, the less angry I felt with time. I knew I was doing the right thing and just wanted to continue on the same path.

Cry If You Feel Like It

Crying is a normal reaction to sadness, pain and sometimes anger too. When you feel things are not in your control, you might feel the need to weep. Crying is a sign that you are hurt and vulnerable. In fact, it is even considered healthy, as it cleans your eyes of any bacteria and dirt. Despite the benefits, you shouldn't force yourself to cry, thinking once you cry, you will feel better. It has to come naturally and when it does, don't hold back on the tears. Don't listen to anyone who tells you that you have to act strong for your family or that the soul of the deceased will be hurt if you continue to weep. It is okay to let go and get it out of your system. Eventually, you are going to feel better after crying. However, if the crying doesn't stop, you might want to talk to somebody about it. According to Judith Orloff, a renowned psychologist and grief counselor, tears are one of the most basic and effective ways of healing (Blessitt & Kathleen, 2018). So if you feel like crying, just let the river flow because it will help jumpstart the process of healing.

Write About the Way You Feel

Writing how you feel is another great way to deal with your anger in a creative and less harmful way. If you are someone who rarely expresses anger openly, journaling the thoughts can be a great way to allow yourself some relief from all the piled up emotions. Journaling your thoughts shows you how you feel and also hints at ways to deal with it. There are a hundred things you can write about. For instance, if you are angry towards the deceased, write them an angry letter and express how you feel now that they are gone. Monica A. Frank, a clinical psychologist, believes that an anger letter is a great way to channel inner rage and acknowledge its existence (Frank, 2004).

Stay Distracted

Distractions such as taking up a new hobby or going for a jog can help clear your mind of the anger you feel and keep it occupied. Doing something you enjoy doing, such as a hobby, reduces the number of stress hormones in your body by producing the feel-good chemical called dopamine. The higher their content in your body, the less angry you will feel.

Forgive Yourself, the Deceased and Others

Sometimes, there is not much that we can do but forgive ourselves, the deceased or anyone linked to the death. It is the hardest thing to do but also the one that frees you. Forgiveness usually comes after one has accepted the loss and understands that there is no point in staying in the past. It is a way of allowing yourself to move past the pain, heartache, and anger. It heals you from within. It mends relationships that might have gone sour after the way you treated them with blame and anger. When I was bereft, I couldn't understand why everyone kept visiting my house every day. Their presence was like a constant reminder of my loss—the one thing that I was trying to get over. Every day when I saw their bleak and sunken faces, I would go back to feeling depressed and feel like a failure.

So one day, I just lashed out and told them not to revisit. What I didn't realize back then was that their intentions were pure. They just wanted to take care of me in my most vulnerable times. After a few days I realized that although their presence made me mad, it also helped me think about other things than my wife. Even if, in my head, I was cursing them, their presence was still keeping my mind off the grief. So in a way, they were actually helping me by just being there. I went to meet them and apologize for my behavior. I asked for forgiveness and in return got the warmest hugs.

The point is, don't hold grudges. What's done has been done. There is no going back from where you are right now, no matter how much you try. So how about forgiving yourself, the dead and others for the sake of your own sanity?

Dealing with Guilt and Regret—I Wish I Could Have Done Something

Like anger, guilt is another persistent and commonly occurring emotion during mourning. Did you know that guilt and regret are two different emotions? For all we know, you might be trying to treat a completely different emotion all this time. Therefore, what you need is some clarity before trying to address this issue using techniques and strategies that work.

Guilt happens when we are in the middle of doing something and realize that we are doing it wrong. It is usually linked with legal, ethical or moral reasons. For instance, if you see someone being bullied and see it as a wrong thing, that is guilt you feel. There is a chance for you to overcome it right then and there by standing up to the bully. However, if you choose not to and go home thinking about it and later feel sorry for the kid and ashamed at yourself, that is regret. The opportunity to do something about it has passed and you are left with nothing that you can do or say that will make things better.

Regret is experienced when we look back at our actions and feel ashamed because nothing more can be done about it.

But no matter how you put it, both these emotions do make you feel worse in the end, don't they? Especially when talking in the context of bereavement, there isn't anything you can do about the situation even if you knew about it all along. For instance, if your loved one suffered through a chronic illness, there wasn't much you could have done to change the state they were in. So you basically end up feeling both guilt and regret at the same time which is just a way to torture yourself.

The reason for this explanation is crucial because our goal is to help you come out of it. When you know what you are going through, you seek specific means to resolve it. When we feel guilty about something, there is a chance to make things right (if possible), such as seeking forgiveness, making reparations and the like. Conversely, when dealing with regret, the work you need to put in revolves more around forgiveness, acceptance and moving on.

During the time of grief and bereavement, we often find ourselves constantly on trial for the "should haves" and "could haves." We blame ourselves for not going to the doctor sooner, not noticing the signs or not paying enough attention to know that someone is depressed. We ourselves become the judge and jury and very easily put ourselves into the prison of self-regret and guilt. What we fail to see is that everything isn't black or white. There is also some grey.

So why do we experience this immense guilt when deep down we know that we weren't to blame?

One of the many hypotheses suggests that the reason we feel like this is that we have always been told to focus on the future, live for it or plan it. And when we do plan it, we don't account for such incidents in our perfect little scenarios. The human mind loves balance in everything. It loves peace. It gets anxious when something unexpected happens and ruins all our plans. Then, the need to rewind and start all over again is what causes chaos. Everything has to be planned from scratch again, which is something that our mind is not too great at. On any given day, when asked to imagine what life would be like, we have a routine explanation for it. We all get up in the morning, have breakfast, head off to work, come back, have dinner and then go to sleep. Somewhat robotic, this is what our brain digs—the normal.

Why do so many of us experience overwhelming guilt when rationally we know we are not to blame? When asked to imagine how the next day would be, the brain concocts pretty much the same image again. But it all comes collapsing down when death occurs. It shatters the perfect world we have created for ourselves and our families.

The mind goes haywire and doesn't understand how to cope with it. According to it, there has to be someone to blame for all this. This is when we lose control. Why? Because our mind needs answers. It needs to make sense of this senselessness.

Getting Over Guilt

So now that we understand where guilt stems from, the next rational step is to look at ways to address it in the right manner.

Acknowledge It

Like anger, guilt also needs to be acknowledged first. Guilt isn't something we feel all the time in our daily routines. It isn't something we come to terms with every day. This makes it harder for us to handle or manage it in the first place. If this is the first time you are grieving the loss of someone dear to you, you must be going through many unfamiliar emotions, guilt being one of them. So the first step is to identify what it is and acknowledge its existence. Don't try to avoid coming to terms with it by distracting yourself with other things. If you are feeling guilty, then this means that there are some underlying issues that need addressing. As human beings, it is very easy for our brains to focus on the bad things we do instead of the good ones. So there will be feelings of shame, doubt, failure, and insecurity during bereavement.

Seek Support From Others

Feeling guilty or like a failure can sometimes draw you away from people who care about you. You might think they will judge you for being a poor partner, sibling, friend or parent but it isn't like that. Anyone who is there by your side is there because they want to support you and help you through the process of grieving. So instead of pushing them away, seek their support and talk to them about how you are feeling. Chances are they will help you overcome the guilt. If not, hopefully, they will leave you with some valuable advice about counseling or therapy that will help you heal faster.

When we lose loved ones, we think that no one in the world misses them more than we do. Again, that's a wrong assumption. If there has been a death in the family, everyone will be more or less equally in pain and grieving. So why go through it alone and not as a group. Why not talk about the things that upset you? Firstly, it will be much easier to cope with it when you come to the realization that others feel the same way as you. Then, together you can all find inner peace and help each other heal through the grieving process. Secondly, when you realize you aren't the only one going through all this, then you will also accept that what you are feeling is completely normal and nothing to worry about.

Think Positively

Easier said than done, looking on the bright side and focusing on the present can truly be a game-changer. The goal should be to put a cap on all the negative thinking and not let it get to your brain. One technique that can help you cope with the negative and harmful thoughts is commanding your mind to just stop thinking about them altogether. This technique, called "thought stopping," works when you are fully determined to take control of your body and mind. Saying stop and busying yourself with something or just getting up and going for a walk can clear your head and allow it to focus on other things around you.

If the thoughts still persist, try to turn them into positive and realistic thoughts. For example, if someone you loved died after a prolonged and painful disease, how about thinking of it as a positive thing since now they are in a much better and pain-free state. Isn't it better to not see them in pain anymore or watch them cry? Isn't it less stressful now that you don't have to keep rushing to the hospital in the middle of the night? Isn't it less painful than seeing their skin injected with cannulas? It is, isn't it?

When my wife died, I blamed myself for many days. But once I joined a support group and heard about the pain others had to go through with their loved ones, the piling medical bills, sleepless nights, praying, visiting one doctor after the other, I realized how easy it had been for me. My wife passed away in his sleep. How hard was that? At least I didn't have to watch the life fade out of her eyes for months. At least I didn't have to give up my job to stay at home and care for her all day.

So I started viewing it as a positive thing. It would have broken my heart to see her in pain.

Learn To Let Go

Even if you had done everything right, there was still a chance that everything would have ended the way it did. The thing is, we believe there is nothing that isn't in our control. After all, we are at the top of the chain with a brain that works miracles. But there are some things that are never in anyone's control. The sooner we realize this, the sooner we learn to let go of the things pulling us down. We learn to free ourselves from the emotions of guilt and shame when we comprehend that some things are just going to be and there is not much you can do about them. So try to focus on forgiveness and acceptance.

Dealing With Jealousy—Why Is Everyone Acting So Normal So Suddenly?

A few months after the death of my wife, I happened to stumble upon a conversation of my fellow colleagues who were talking about how uncaring or controlling their wives were. One husband lamented how his wife never appreciates the little things he does around the house and just keeps on complaining and nagging. She is too busy to attend to the needs of his kids or take out time for them. Do you know what I wanted to do then? I wanted to just punch him in the face and remind him of how ungrateful he was being. I would give everything in my power just to have my wife nag at me once. At least she would be there!

Before that, there had only been a few instances when I felt jealous of other couples walking out of a movie theater holding hands or fathers taking care of their kids and playing with them in the backyard. I envied what they had and secretly cried over my loss.

Had my wife passed away when our hair was all white and we walked with the help of a cane, I think the loss would have been less severe. After all, you expect death at that age. You are also somewhat prepared for it. But I lost my wife when she wasn't even in her forties. Young, full of life, caring and devoted—which made it so much harder. I had no answers to why or what had happened. Now that I look back at my past state, I guess that is how you are supposed to overcome your loss. I am not proud of the way I dealt with it; but I definitely am proud of the fact that I overcame it.

The reason I am sharing this with you is that I can imagine how you must be feeling right now. It doesn't matter who you lost; seeing others happy and taking things for granted makes us all jealous. We want to have everything in life. We crave more for things that we don't have and others have, be it a luxurious car, a two-story bungalow, a closet full of clothes or friends and family who love us. The sad part is that those who have these don't appreciate their value until they are gone. I guess I am guilty of doing that too. I wish I could have told my wife that I loved her more often. I wish I had cuddled, kissed, hugged, and appreciated more... Now that I can't, every time I see someone with the chance to tell their partners but don't tell them because they think they already know, it just makes me a little mad.

Being ungrateful often comes tagged with feelings of jealousy. The very connotation of the word is horrible. Instantly, it evokes feelings of hatred, mean spirits and negativity. None of us wants to be called that, but how about for once we agree that we are all a little jealous in life? It is an ugly emotion but also very human. After all, it is also the same emotion that breeds motivation and fuels us with conviction to do things we never thought we would.

Although it is normal to feel a little jealous when grieving the death of someone, you must also understand that excess of any emotion can harm your mind, body and even relationships. The biggest drawback, however, is that jealousy can slow down the process of healing and keep dragging you back to the stages of grief you have already escaped. So you have to be extra careful when dealing with jealousy, as you don't want to start all over again or go back to being depressed.

Coping With Jealousy

Coping with jealousy isn't hard. Of course, it will take some time to stop resenting what others have and you don't, but it will happen. There will come a day when you will be able to look at others and celebrate their joys and happiness with them. Below are some helpful tips to get over being jealous.

Understand What It Is

Are you feeling jealousy or envy? Used synonymously, these two terms are slightly different from one another. Envy relates to the desire to acquire something another person has whereas jealousy is related to something that has been lost already. So are you being envious or jealous? In the beginning, you will be more envious. When you reach the stage of bargaining, this envy turns into jealousy.

Once you have moved past that distinction, you also need to identify if what you are feeling is normal or irrational.

Normal jealousy allows you to self-evaluate and improve. It entails learning about your insecurities and dealing with them accordingly.

Irrational jealousy, on the other hand, is jealousy without any factual relevance. You feel jealous for no apparent reason. This is more of a lingering than just a normal feeling and people who experience this type of jealousy often engage in negative behaviors. They are determined to keep finding faults within themselves and others without actually doing anything about them. Think of it as crying over spilled milk without taking any initiative to change the way you feel.

Focus on Your Actions, Not Emotions

If you accidentally express your jealousy, be responsible enough to apologize. Remember the situation with my colleagues discussing their wives's failings? I so wanted to give them a piece of my mind. Had I done so, it would have been wrong on my part. Sometimes, knowing that your words will affect someone's mood and feelings in a negative way, it is better to get it out of your system in a more suitable and less hurtful manner. Therefore, focus on your actions wisely.

Reevaluate Your Jealousy

Don't see yourself as a jealous person. Instead, think of yourself as partially happy. True, you lost someone you loved and it makes you sad, but split your ego in a way that enables you to feel happy for them instead of jealous. For example, you can feel happy for others because they don't have to go through what you did.

Avoid Situations That Trigger Jealousy

During the first few months after the death, it is best to avoid situations and places that trigger your anger. For instance, you might want to pass on some holiday invitations if you think that accepting them will be too much for you to handle. Certain places and situations become a strong reminder of your loss. For example, if you two met at your parents' house or have many memories in that space, going there will only trigger further grief and anger if you haven't recovered completely. You deserve some time off to heal properly, as unresolved grief can lead to depression.

Avoid Lashing Out at Others

Don't take out your jealousy and anger on others. They may be taking things for granted—things you wished would return to you—but you have no right to lash out toward them with your hatred and anger. You will feel overwhelmed by your feelings, but don't let them overpower you. Expressing your anger and resentment negatively will damage your relationships with others, and believe me when I tell you this—you are going to need all the support you can to process through all the stages of grief and loss.

Log Off Social Media for Some Time

Doesn't everyone on social media look like the happiest individual on earth? Social media sites are bound to make you feel insecure and sad about your life. Someone will always be having a baby, getting married, graduating, vacationing or celebrating a new promotion. Although we should celebrate their joy, we often begin to compare their lives with ours. What we don't realize is that a lot of what we see is just fake. Everyone has a set of problems and burdens they are carrying. A picture doesn't tell the whole story. Alas, it is too easy to fall into the trap and feel inferior. If you have friends and family on social media, it can be hard for you to see them moving on and enjoying their lives while you grieve. Again, it comes down to avoiding spaces that trigger jealousy. Stay logged off for a few days or weeks until you are ready to step back into the world.

Talk to Someone About It

Seek professional help if you have a hard time managing your jealousy. Therapists who deal with patients recovering from the loss of death and bereavement can offer some advice and tips on how to move on past your anger and jealousy and begin to view the world from a different, much happier perspective.

4 UNRESOLVED GRIEF—WHEN IT DOESN'T BETTER

No doubt the loss of a loved one is a traumatic and tragic incident, the memories of which will never leave us. They are with us when we lay down in bed and also when we wake up. The first few months when the mourner is trying to get things back to normal again are the hardest. However, with time, eventually everything does get better. But this isn't the case with everyone. Some people just never fully grieve. They keep on clinging to the hope of their loved ones returning to them. They fear that if they stop, if they accept that a loved one is long gone, this bubble they are living in with their loved one will break. That mostly happens with mothers grieving infants after a miscarriage or seniors who have spent several decades together.

But grief should only be transitory. It shouldn't be a permanent state. Acceptance should come, no matter how much time the mourner takes. If it continues to persist and you find yourself weeping uncontrollably even when several weeks or months have passed, then you may be suffering from unresolved or complicated grief.

Understanding Complicated or Unresolved Grief

Complicated, incomplete or unresolved grief refers to grief that never ends or loses its intensity. It is a medically recognized condition in which the bereaved continues to feel pain that interferes with her ability to function normally. The pain of the loss is so intense and debilitating that it leaves the mourner hopeless of ever recovering from it. Although only 10% of mourners experience such grief, it is still crucial to understand and notice the signs if you think you or someone in your circle is suffering from it. Complicated grief can turn into depression and can be life-threatening.

In other words, you can think of it as a constant state of denial where the mourner doesn't want to accept that death has happened. They will tell you that they still see, smell or sense the presence of their beloved and that he/she hasn't died. Keep in mind that this is a form of disorder and often accompanied with adjustment disorder, substance abuse, PTSD and chronic depression.

Before we learn about the many signs and symptoms of unresolved grief, it is important that we understand the distinction between normal and complicated grief.

Characteristics	Normal Grief	Complicated Grief
Response to Support	Responds to support and comfort	Isn't ready to accept comfort and support from others
Expression of Feelings	Is usually expressive about how they feel (angry, sad, in pain, etc.)	Complains and shows irritation but doesn't express emotions
Outlook towards life	Experiences moments of joy and happiness over time	Demonstrates an all-pervading sense of doom
Perceived Emotions	Displays feelings of emptiness and sadness	Displays constant hopelessness
Expression of Guilt	Expresses guilt but overcomes it with time	Finds it impossible to forgive self over the loss
Intensity of Pain	Decreases with time	Remains constant
Duration	A few weeks or months	Never-ending depression
Self-esteem	Loses self-confidence for some time	Long and deep ongoing loss of confidence

When grief remains unresolved, it can emerge in the form of negative and self-harming thoughts such as suicide.

Signs and Symptoms of Unresolved Grief

Initially, it is impossible to differentiate between normal grief and complicated grief. However, with time, there are some symptoms that are enough to raise red flags. These symptoms include:

- Sadness: The severity of sadness doesn't change over time with unresolved grief. They keep on crying for hours at a time over the loss and don't accept comfort and support.
- Reminders: Even the most beautiful memories turn into painful reminders that the mourner just keeps on playing on repeat.
- Treatments: Common methods of treating grief such as getting busy, going on with day-to-day activities, etc. don't help alleviate the pain and suffering.
- Avoidance: The mourner refuses to accept help from others and prefers to remain isolated and detached from the things happening around her.
- Fear: Mourners become fearful of creating new relationships with anyone as they think they will leave also.
- Avoiding the subject of death: Some people just pretend and do not talk about the accident altogether. They try to push it out of their memories by never recalling it.
- Unwilling to acknowledge: This usually takes the drastic form of the mourner living in a world of her own with her loved ones and pretending that they are still here. Basically, this is a form of not accepting death.
- Irritability and anger: Mourners feel irritated over the smallest things and lose their tempers. They resort to actions like pushing and pulling others without even realizing what they are doing.
- Suicidal thoughts: The mourner keeps talking about how he wishes to be with his loved one or how terrible this life is without her. Such comments can come through hints expressing that there is no purpose to live anymore, etc.
- Intense bitterness: There is also a lack of sympathy for others. People with unresolved grief often discard others' feelings as shallow while they think their loss is the most important one.
- Panic attacks: With unresolved grief, it is common to have panic attacks when talking about death or watching it on TV. A related condition is fear of going to the hospital and becoming anxious at the sound of an ambulance in the distance.

- Guilt and resentment: Self-blaming for what happened and a persistent feeling of regret and resentment lingers with them.
- Obsession with the deceased: Such obsession can show up in repeated calls to the deceased's phone number, talking to her, waiting for her to come home, not getting rid of her used clothes, etc.
- Addiction: Addiction can take various forms, but it typically shows up as self-harming behavior, such as drinking excessively, binge eating, taking drugs or trying out dangerous activities like mountain climbing or underwater diving.
- Numbness and apathy: Those with unresolved grief experience an emotional numbness towards everything. They have a "why bother?" attitude. They also have poor levels of energy or enthusiasm towards things.
- Retaining mundane routines: The fear of change keeps them from trying new things. They prefer to keep things as they are.
- Isolation: Isolated mourners avoid going out or visiting a relative's house during the holidays. They feel detached and think that no one understands them or what they are going through.
- Phobias: Some bereaved can suffer from new phobias, especially ones about their health. For instance, if their loved ones died from a health condition like cancer or pneumonia, they become overly cautious about developing the same illness. They become extra careful about their diets and start to believe that the disease too.
- Loss of interests: Like all of these symptoms, any are likely for a relatively short period of time following the death of a loved one. But when a mourner permanently loses interest in the things he previously enjoyed doing or spending time on, he probably is struggling with complicated grief. For instance, he might act careless about the needs of his pets, stop writing or painting, etc.
- Taking risks: Risk-taking is a common symptom among teens going through grief. They deliberately begin indulging in risky and life-threatening behaviors to feel the adrenaline rush. These behaviors can include things like rash driving, jumping off a moving vehicle or taking drugs.
- Fear of loss: A constant fear persists. They think the world isn't safe. Consequently, they are hyper-alert all of the time. Even the slightest of sounds wakens them or causes them to go into a state of panic. This is very common among mourners whose loved ones died in a fire, accident, mugging or burglary incident. They keep

rechecking the locks on the door, keep the windows shut and curtains down and don't step out of the house unless required.

Learning To Cope With It

The biggest challenge with unresolved or incomplete grief is that it doesn't get resolved with typical strategies. For example, trying to overcome complicated grief by engaging yourself in routine activities won't be as effective as it would be when dealing with symptoms of normal grief. Complicated grief requires professional intervention and help. Since it is a disorder and not just a temporary phase, those who develop it need treatment to get better. Especially if someone has resorted to harmful behaviors such as drinking, becoming a workaholic or using drugs to momentarily forget about the pain, therapies mentioned below are recommended.

1. **Psychotherapy:** Many therapists, after reviewing the severity of the depression and inability to carry on with routine tasks and chores, suggest psychotherapy. It is a well-tested treatment whose goals are to help mourners return to functioning like they did before the death of a loved one. Think of it as an intervention to promote recovery. This form of therapy can help the bereaved to identify the hurdles in overcoming their grief by drawing connections with the lost individuals. Two of the most prominent types of psychotherapies include Interpersonal Psychotherapy and Complicated Grief Therapy.

2. **Interpersonal psychotherapy** aims to help the grieving detach from unhealthy and obsessive behaviors as well as form better relationships. The therapist helps the mourner past each stage of loss with guidance and help with their pain. The goal is to rekindle their interest in life again and become a better and more resourceful human being like before. This is achieved by evoking memories of the deceased and the events around the death. The therapist also touches on subjects like anger, resentment, and regrets associated with death. The bereft are reassured that what they are experiencing is normal and quite common, which makes them feel less of a freak. Finally, they receive recommended exercises, medications and activities to keep them engaged and moving forward.

3. **Grief Monitoring Diary:** This form of therapy includes the

therapist instructing the mourner to jot down how they feel and log their experiences each week. They are asked to note down the highs and lows of the week and what feelings they felt. For instance, if the mourner visited a family gathering of friends and family, how did it feel? Did it feel weird, comfortable or even sadder than before after coming back? The goal of a grief monitoring diary is to identify the emotional triggers and thoughts that cause unrest. The therapist reviews the diary each week and determines a course of action.

4. **Motivational interviewing** is another form of the recommended therapy for people battling unresolved grief. It focuses on how we all are capable of making positive changes in our lives. It helps mourners achieve those changes using a set of practices and exercises. It also demonstrates the harmful impact of negative behaviors and how harmful habits can be turned into positive habits.

5. **Creative techniques**, as the name suggests, are different from the usual in-the-clinic therapies. These usually involve activities and interests like art therapy, journal writing, starting blogs, memory bracelets or songwriting. Ideally, whichever form of art or creative hobby the mourner finds most pleasing and comforting is what is suggested. The talking in most of the sessions involves showing what they have done so far. For example, the therapist might ask the mourner to show if they have been writing their journal or painting. It is more of a unique form of treatment that allows you to express your feelings in the form of art. You can use it to either talk about your grief or celebrate the life of the departed.

5 OVERCOMING GRIEF… HOW TO GO ON LIVING

Whichever stage of grief you are going through, there are many ways to get past it and speed the process of healing. Although there is no rush, it is always in your best interests to overcome the grief and revive your life. Of course, it is easier said than done and difficult to even think about it, but you just have to. You have to put one foot after the other and accept the loss. Even if you feel shattered into a gazillion pieces, there is still hope that things will turn for the good. Isn't it the only good thing in life right now? Hope?

In this last part of the book, we shall discover and work through strategies and techniques that will help a bereaved person like yourself feel normal again. Adopting them will take some effort and willingness on your part, but trust me—if you are ready to come out of the painful situation you are in right now, you will! That is my promise to you. There isn't any hard and fast rule to following all of these. The reason I am listing so many of them is that I want you to pick the ones you can adopt and leave the rest for some other day.

All in all, I want you to snap out of your pain and believe that there is more to life than just grieving. See how beautiful the world is and how important the people in it are.

Strategies To Cope With the Pain

Before I get onto the strategies, I want to make one thing very clear. Although these exercises and practices will help you recover from your loss, it is still time that will cause the most healing. As clichéd as it sounds, time does most of the healing. It is the one thing that takes away the pain step by step. You are going to feel whole one day and look at your present self and appreciate how far you have come. Something good comes out of everything. We may not understand it today, but we surely will tomorrow, a month or a year from now.

So let time work its magic and heal you.

Seek Support

The first and foremost thing I want you to do is to accept the comfort, support, and empathy you are receiving. Everyone who calls to check on you, keeps visiting your house or does something to help you recover is someone who dearly loves you and wants to help you. So don't hush them, push them away or seek isolation. If accepting help makes you feel like a weak person and you wish to recover on your own, hear me when I tell you that there is no harm in accepting help. It doesn't make you less of a person. This hesitancy is very common among men. They don't want the hugs, the comforting talk and help around the house. They think of themselves as too tough to accept help. But there is no shame in it. Grief is a common and natural process. Talking to someone about your loss keeps you sane. It limits all the negative thoughts and distracts us from our grief, even if for only a few hours at a time. Find someone to support you and remind you that there still is a bright side to look at. Find someone who will walk with you, sit on a bench with you and not utter a single word. Find someone who will help around the house without asking and not make it sound like a big favor. Find someone who will talk you through the stage you are going through and suggest means to get by.

Where does support come from?

Friends

True friends will always understand what you are going through. Even when they haven't experienced such a loss, they still know you and if they notice that you need some emotional assistance, they will be more than willing to offer it to you. You just have to accept it. Talk to them about the emotions you are experiencing and the thoughts in your head. Chances are, they will offer you valuable advice and also stay with you to see you through it.

Family

Leaning on your family members for support is another great way to recover from bereavement. Since they too lost someone dear to them, it will be easier to connect with them on multiple levels and cope with the loss together. You can each lift one another out of the darkest pit and comprehend the emotions better. They will offer you a shoulder to cry on without questioning. At least, that is what happened to me. My wife's family were the first ones to comfort me and stayed by my side throughout. Even though my wife and her family weren't that close, I still remember her mother calling me every other day to check on me and the kids and drop by whenever she was in the area just to talk about my wife's childhood memories and her happiest moments. Soon, it became a ritual we held every week and together we helped each other through it. After all, she too lost a daughter.

Support Groups

If you find no comfort amongst friends and family, how about finding it in a support group? They prove to be extremely beneficial because they not only allow the bereft to see that she isn't the only one grieving a loss, but such groups also connect people struggling with similar losses. For example, if you are grieving the loss of a child or parent, someone in a support group will also be grieving the same. The two of you can share your stories and find peace together. Every neighborhood has a support group available. You can contact a local hospital or counseling center near your house and get referred to one. If you think that the burden of the loss is too much to handle on your own, join a support group for help. They offer more than just a regular chit-chat session, like the ones we see in lots of movies.

Online Forums

The reason I am adding this to my list is that I have been on multiple forums and talked about my loss openly only to find out that there are many others on the same journey. I received messages of encouragement, prayers and warm wishes from people across the globe. On the darkest days, reading them offered me the strength I lacked and helped me continue to move forward. I am sure you will find help online too. Also, there are tons of helpful guides and books that talk you through the process of grieving in detail, so they can also be resourceful.

Find Distractions

Distractions allow our minds to divert from the persistent thoughts we surround ourselves with throughout the time of grieving. It is time you put an end to the what-if scenarios in your head. What's done is done. There is no reversing it. What you need now is to return to living the life you were living before this awful incident. Staying distracted doesn't mean to completely forget about your loss and pretend that it didn't happen. It is allowing your mind something refreshing to think about for once. How about you indulge in any of these activities, to begin with?

Volunteer

One of the best ways to cope with personal loss is by helping others. But how can you contribute, you may ask? There are many things you can do to make a positive difference in someone's life. You can always offer donations, but I personally am fond of contributing my time. Visit a nursing home, pet shelter or a home for special kids. Give them the gift of your time and see how uplifting and peaceful the whole experience is. When we feel we are serving the greater good, it automatically reduces some of the guilt we feel internally. There are hundreds and thousands of people needing help. Some are starving, some are suffering through unspeakable diseases, and some have been bereaved like yourself. Spending time with them and having a heart-to-heart conversation with them is what you need.

It serves as the perfect distraction and comes with a greater reward—inner peace.

Go on a Vacation

Spending some time away from the normal routine and your familiar environment can be an excellent means to keep yourself distracted. Book a flight to someplace where you had always wanted to visit. If the finances don't allow, plan a road trip with your friends and go exploring. If no one has the time for it, then go camping alone. Not only will it take your mind elsewhere, but it will also offer some peaceful time to gather your scattered thoughts. A change of environment will also lift your mood and allow you to taste freedom. It may feel odd to even think about such a thing while grieving, but a weekend away doesn't make a big difference and it's definitely not something that will raise eyebrows. After all, you are just trying to cope with your loss. Everyone who loves you dearly should be okay with it and appreciate you for taking the initiative.

Join a New Class/Course

It can be anything from HIIT, knitting or skiing… The point is to offer you a form of distraction that you enjoy. If you have a passion for something, say playing chess or horseback riding, how about joining a course or taking a class every now and then? This will not only get you out of the house but also amongst people who share the same passion as you. Not to mention, it will take your mind elsewhere for a little while and lift your mood.

Become Social Again

Maybe this isn't something to do right away, but staying isolated has never done anyone any good. If anything, it only adds to the pain because there just isn't much to think about other than your loss. If you have been avoiding going out, visiting friends or going to family gatherings because you think it will be too hurtful, hold that thought right there.

There are tons of benefits to breaking through your routine life. Spending time with friends and family can help you cope with the loss faster. Of course, some places where you used to go with the deceased will be challenging to handle, but how about you reminisce over the good times you had with them there and not about the fact that they are missing? It's all about perspective and if you continue to look at the darker side of things, you are only going to make it harder for you to come out of it.

Pursue New Hobbies and Interests

Do something you have been meaning to do before this incident happened and changed everything. Engaging in hobbies and interests that you are passionate about can keep you engaged. Perhaps you had always wanted to learn to hike, paint like a pro or own a small auto repair shop for your love for cars, but you never did. Now is the time to do it. It will keep you busy and also offer a few hours of me-time.

Emotional Strategies

There is nothing wrong with experiencing the pain of losing someone. Surely it hurts, but such pain is natural. Remember, a diamond goes through a lot to turn into the most adored stone in the world. You too are going to take a beating that comes in the form of inexpressible pain—pain so harsh that you think your heart is going to explode with it.

Grieve fully.

Coping with our emotions only comes when they are in our control. That control isn't possible when the loss is new and sudden. React to the emotions naturally and when you are done, incorporate the techniques mentioned below to feel better about yourself.

Cry

Cry if the burden seems too hard to carry. Cry until you can't cry anymore. There is normally a stigma attached to crying men. They are supposed to act tough and just get it over with because crying is for the weak and they are strong. At least, that is what most men are taught since infancy. But crying isn't a sign of weakness, as often perceived; it is also a great way to release any anger, guilt, resentment or regret from your system.

It is a guarantee that you will feel a hundred times better afterward than when you kept it all inside of you. It lifts off the burden and makes you feel lighter. It can also help with clearing your head. So don't look at it as something bad or negative. Don't care about what others will think or say.

Avoid Grief Triggers

Triggers can be places, situations, events or important milestones. Some people have a hard time attending events such as holiday dinners because they remind them of who's missing. Some spend their anniversaries locked in their rooms because they are too painful to handle. Triggers can reawaken memories of the lost loved one, which is why you must manage them tactfully. You don't want to go back to feeling miserable after attending an event because you missed having your loved one beside you. The triggers will make you emotionally weak but that is quite normal considering the state you are in. If you wish to not feel miserable, plan ahead on how you are going to cope with them. I am sure others will understand where you are coming from.

Treasure the Good Times

Understandably, the things the deceased left behind are now the closest to your heart. They are the only reminders you have of them. How about viewing them as something to cherish? If there are many pictures of the two of you together, how about making a collage of them or putting them all in a scrapbook? You can also create a video of those pictures or record stories of everyone and what they have to say about the departed. Assuredly, it is one of the most creative ways to keep their memories for a lifetime.

Honor the Deceased

If you wish to remember them always, how about doing something that will honor them and their memory? For instance, if they talked about doing something like volunteering at the nearest senior's home or watching a game live, how about you do that on their behalf? Surely, if they are watching over you, they will love you for it. Also, it will bring joy so reassuring that it will be hard to put into words. My wife always talked about how much she would like to donate to the foster care center in her town where she grew up. Some of her closest friends growing up were from that center. So when I didn't know what to do with all her clothes, shoes, perfumes and cosmetics, I just put them all in a carton and sent it to that foster home. It felt so comforting to receive the warmest "thank you" card made by the kids around Christmas.

Forgive Yourself

This can't be stressed enough. You have to forgive yourself or else you will never overcome your loss. Forgiveness is the route to diminished anguish. There is nothing you could have done to prevent this death and you didn't deserve it. But it happened and there is no going back, is there? So why do you keep torturing yourself with things that were never in your control? Learn to let go. You can't alter something that has already transpired. Why beat yourself up about it?

Take Care of Yourself

As discussed in part 2 of the book, the emotional turmoil of your loss can leave you feeling stressed, drained and weak. This is why it is important to take extra care of your health so that you don't fall sick physically. This includes:

Eating Right and Wholesomely

The very thought of food during bereavement is the last thing on one's mind, but you must understand that your body needs the energy to get you through. The first few days will be the toughest with all the arrangements for the funeral and receiving of guests, so you must stay in good shape and have your energy levels up. Continue to eat nutrient-rich foods in the first few weeks after the death as you are continuously thinking about death. Don't give in to the temptation to binge eat on comfort food. It will offer some relief but will only be detrimental in the long run.

Exercising To Stay Fit

Physical health is as important as mental health. Engaging in physical activity helps with overcoming grief and loss. It will keep you distracted as well as make you feel better as you leave the house and walk in the fresh air. If you aren't a big fan of the gym, try going for a walk or jog every day for half an hour. If you are filled with anger and resentment, there are also activities like golfing, hitting a punching bag or shooting bottles at a shooting academy to release anger and frustration.

Sleeping for 7 to 8 Hours

Your mind also rests when you rest and it definitely needs a break from all the thinking during the day. Sleeping also helps the brain make sense of the things that happened throughout the day. Not getting enough sleep means depriving the brain of that consolidation time and will result in your waking up feeling fatigued and groggy. Believe me, it will be harder to get through the day when you haven't slept well. So make sure you are getting some quality sleep every night so that you are mentally and physically ready to manage your grief.

Meditating

Meditation and yoga, like exercising, are great ways to release bad thoughts and behaviors from your system. They can teach you how to cope with your loss by taking control of your mind and by choosing the best techniques to manage it.

CONCLUSION

"And can it be that in a world so full and busy the loss of one creature makes a void so wide and deep that nothing but the width and depth of eternity can fill it up!"

I like to think that Charles Dickens had it figured out. He knew of the pain that hits us like a wave when faced with the unexpected death. He knew of the void that is created and how wide it is that no matter what you put into it, it still feels empty. He understood how important loving a person can be. He knew how much time it can take to fill that void and move on.

They say, until you are in someone's shoes you can't imagine their pain. I have never read anything truer than that. All those years, after attending one funeral after the other and visiting friends to comfort them in their time of grieving, you never really feel the emotion until it happens to you.

While I planned out this book, every little memory with my dear wife danced in front of my eyes. All those examples I used or left out were stories we both created together. From the day we got married to the last goodnight before bed, I cherish everything wholeheartedly. There isn't anything in the world that I would not give just to have one moment with her again. But I know that she isn't coming back and neither is the one you lost.

The reason I titled this book the bereavement code and not some random, "While you are gone" or "How to live without you" theme is because I strongly believe that we all have our own stories to tell, our own heart to mend, our own grief to deal with and our own hopes to cling to.

It is like each of us has a different code that unlocks how we deal with the grief. The code is unique in all aspects. It isn't bound by any timeline or a standardized technique that works as a universal key. It is only yours to keep and yours to use. How you choose to use it is up to you.

My only hope is that you do!.